Billboards, Murals, Signs & Street Banners of Chicago

Ekphrastic Poems
Mark Fishbein

Table of Contents

for my Zoom poet friends

Authors note:

All the pictures used here are taken from my cellphone, often when driving. They were all made available to the public for public consumption. I consumed them with poetry.

The poems are offered in the order they were written.

All cities offer their share of prompts for ekphrastic poetry. I moved to Chicago about a year ago, having lived in New York, Paris, and Washington DC. Something clicked, and I started hunting out billboards for inspiration, which spread out to the ample street art. Projects like this can go on endlessly. Each prompt invites a different voice, and a different stance. It is very serious fun.

Mark Fishbein
January, 2024

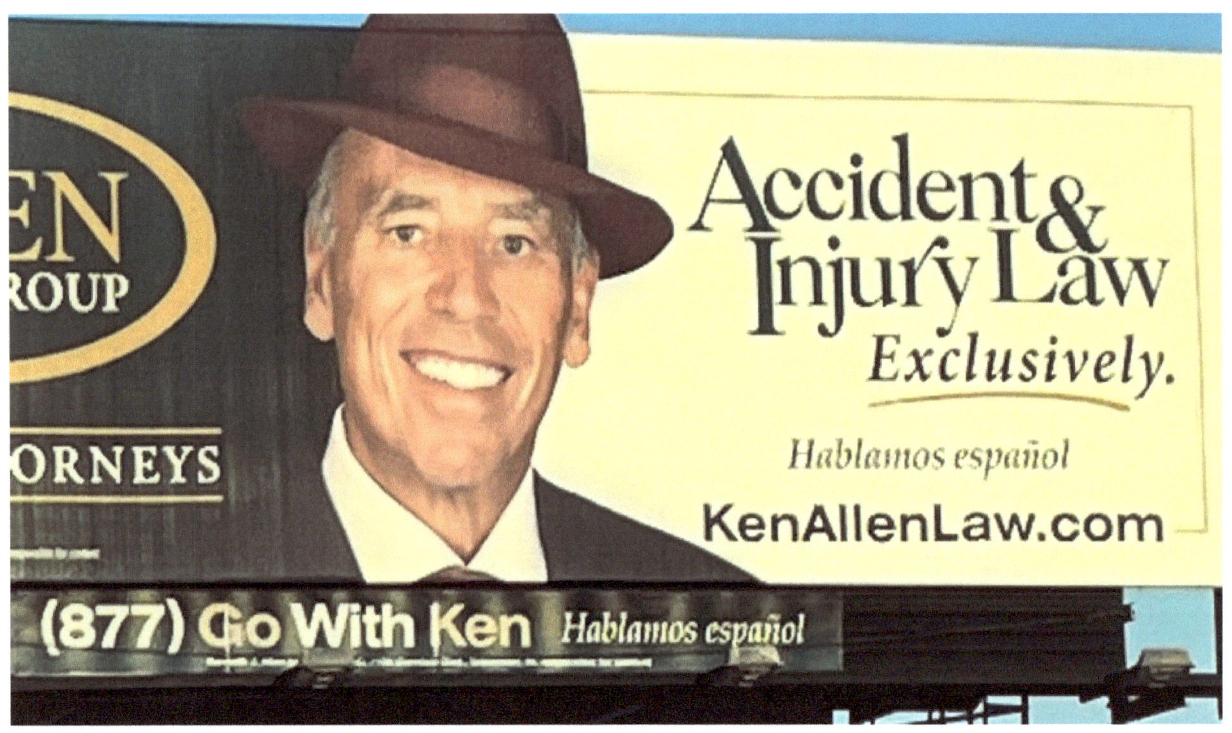
EN
ROUP
ORNEYS
Accident&
Injury Law
Exclusively.
Hablamos español
KenAllenLaw.com
(877) Go With Ken   Hablamos español

Go with Ken

Ken Allen, lawyer, who *yo hablo español*
Forever charming the endless schools of trucks and cars
On the route I-90 Toll Road.
Every time I pass you and the ingenious way
Your hat pops above the billboard
I think of various personas:

The singer in Paris, 1940, a Charles Trenet.
The voice of fado in Pessoa's Lisbon.
The Scottish tenor who drives you to tears with
The Bonnie Banks o' Loch Lomond.
Sometimes I see you as a Jewish comedian
In the 1950's Blue Room at the Concord Hotel,
Or a second for Simon Templar, the Saint,
Or a Hollywood cha-cha teacher
In the reign of Xavier Cugat.

But no, instead, you might be the slimiest bastard
I've come across in years,
With that sleezy snake oil salesman smile
Who would use an ingrown toenail
To sue for a million bucks,
And I've noticed everyone who passes
Gives you and that fucking hat you wear
The finger.

SKIMS
FEAT. ROSALÍA
CLEAR CHANNEL
006078
PARKING FOR
Midwe
Express C

belly button

at the same hour on the daily commute
she waits for me on chicago avenue
calling me to her belly button
what music coming from this cave
trumpets and samba drums
await my tongue
i will dwell in this land as moses said
when he entered midian from the desert

o beloved america   land of celebrity underwear
every day she stares as i wait at the red light
with twenty seconds worth of hot flashes
in poses from erotic tantra scrolls
this succulent cave awaits me
to fill with rubies and bitcoins

what do you want america
relentless in waving pheromones at me
a sexual animal with acrobatic orgasms

but may the gods be merciful
if my lust becomes unruly
should i tell a passing woman
she has eyes of great beauty

OLD NATIONAL BANK
You're never too old
to Get Old.

sestina to growing old

you're never too old to get old
even if the music you like is old
school and your clothes are older
than old man river   you are the oldest
windbag in the room who remembers olden
days when aging was an abstraction

here's to old time's sake and realizations
same ole same old   the years are golden
we are beginning to sound like old
farts complaining about getting older
since aristotle   bring back the good ol'
days is now the mantra of the nouveau oldies

not so long ago we wore blindfolds
not giving way to the ol' heave ho
to wake each day with fresh contusions
and the bittersweet wisdoms that are old
as methuselah   the same rigmarole
the bartering of memories sold

we said   when we wed   *let's grow old
together*   well we made it to the old
corral with rituals of the same old
salt sprinkled on the golden oldies
to treat each day as resurrection
and pick fruits ripe just ready to mold

soon we'll reach the final threshold
our passing has been foretold
in dead ends of anticipation
we sing our new year's auld
lang syne   danse the old
soft shoe in time's scary scaffold

you're never too old to get old
as father time grows coldly older
with his old cane of resignation

Love Always Wins
CARNIVALE
RESTAURANT • LOUNGE
EST. 2005

Love Always Wins at the Carnivale Restaurant and Lounge

Victory is renowned when dice of loneliness are thrown
Bring cash or credit cards and every bitcoin you own
Prepare to go naked (except for your cellphone)
Bring the hurt you hold deep in your bones
And our orthopedist will inject cortisone
Meet your mate when you come alone
A Debauched Hospodar disowned
Enter straight go home stoned
Laying in a water bed throne
A trip to the palatial zone
Satisfactions on loan
Wear sex cologne
And it's known
Free to groan
Afterglow
Of holy
moan
Oh
O
!

SELF
PARK
TRY
POETRY

try poetry

i try many things
which leads me to keep trying
to find something between
saturday matinee at the opera
& saturday night at the roxy roller rink
i have tried
meditations & psychosomatic deliberations
yoga & and the elite sport of squash
but poetry
yes i still try that too
it makes me break out in rashes
my knees buckle
i end up like an old mop
leaning against a building
a stoned cowboy that has to pee
while my brain flickers with words
like a dizzy swan
a streetlight beaming like a star &
there's no valet to park my car

BEYOND
THE ORIGINAL
ORANGE CHICKEN

beyond the original orange chicken

the saber tooth tiger sings
the woke octopus swoons
whirling dervish wildebeests
dung beetles in recitative
poetry that reeks of kief
red butt baboons   a sushi moon
stegosaurus playing violin
beyond the original orange chicken

giraffes with artificial knees
a gaggle of bees buzz pleasantly
baobab trees with rainbow leaves
tango jellyfish   waltzing vultures
horny urchins   a witch's brew
of prepubescent spider spit
all possible   probable   by definition
beyond the original orange chicken

Skinny dip.
Amazing Pools Category
airbnb
BRANDED CITIES

red light skinny dip

naked   alone   unexpectedly
floating on a mat
in a shallow blue pool that
reaches like a jetty into vastness
of cooled marble prominades
an oasis in another continent
where patches of weeds scatter
to a parched and lifeless horizon
shaded by fast pink clouds
far from the brick-stained skyline

you absorb the dry breeze's
scent of cactus flower
immersed with the slightest waving
of your hands like gentle wings
to guide you on thc tepid water
effortlessly in slow laps

sanctified from the static of traffic
a listless pulse of daily commute

startled by an angry horn
green light
and you are gone

13'-10"
Milwaukee Av
Grand Av
530N
PICCOLO SOGNO

Antipasti Piccolo Sogno

Stuck in traffic where Milwaukee meets Grand,
listening to Pandora on the radio,
something by Vivaldi for castrato and strings....
when right on cue the mural appeared—
the Satyr gets the Sabine in blue;
a post renaissance moment
     when men of muscular myths
had their way with terrified virgins.

How common this little erotic tease
of gods plucking out maidens like flowers—
No royal banquet hall was complete
without galleries filled with statues
in an ecstasy of hungry rape,
to the whips from the violins
and the sonorous counter tenor
whose voice is a tongue between the legs...

People were weird back then.
Buon appetito.

PRIMARK
PRIMARK
KOBRA

Tribute to Muddy

The Blues was becoming wildly popular in 1967. White blues bands like The Blues Project and The Paul Butterfield Blues Band were joining the growing fame of organic black blues singers: John Lee Hooker, Robert Johnson, Bill Bronzy, Howling Wolf, Shaky Jake, Taj Mahal. I was a student at City College New York, and was getting into playing guitar and harmonica. What did I, or any of my peers, white kids from the middle class, have anything in common with what they were singing? Freight trains, mojo monkey paw aphrodisiacs, chain gangs, violence and jealousy from illicit love affairs....

Mr. Waters, sir (may I call you Muddy?), you would not remember me. I was a friend of Paul Osher's cousin, and knew Paul for a while. He was the roommate of Ed Karanja, from Kenya, an exchange student of economics at Columbia University, in 1968. I took his place at the apartment on 122nd street and Amsterdam Avenue. Paul would come around often, play some guitar, have some beers and listen to Karanja tell us of all the girls he was screwing. He had amazing success with the hippie girls he picked up at protest rallies, as Otis Redding or the blues played with the rhythmic bed springs deep into the night.

So the story goes: James Cotton was a genius at the harmonica, he was like an orchestra where a screaming saxophone meets the voice. In 1967 he left to start his own band, and so you needed a fill in.

Now Paul had been playing his mouth harp for years, indistinguishable to Cotton or Little Richard. He heard you were holding auditions at a Greenwich Village club to see what talent was around to fill the void, find a player who played from the gut. Paul gave us a surprise visit the night you chose him and was going on tour, immediately. Paul quit school (he was going to CW Post), and joined your band.

Paul Osher was white, but I kept on thinking he felt the blues like he was black. There is a suffering and a short straw you can't fake about being black in 1967. Paul grew up in Long Island, New York, one of the most segregated communities in the country. He had no fears, no pretentions about being the only white guy in your band. In fact, he told me you never actually discussed it. All the great blues bands were all black. You changed the mold, Muddy; it works both ways.

You will probably not remember that Paul once invited me to come back stage. It was a show at a small club you were playing at when in New York. You and the band were getting ready for the gig with gin or tequila and white powders. The back room was very stark, a few tables and mirrors. I was stoned on pot and beers, and content be a witness of things I'd never seen, only heard about. You were so kind to me, Muddy, you spoke to me through glassy eyes, welcoming any friend of Paul's as a friend of yours. You hadn't even started your set and your face was covered with sweat. I shook your hand. It was moist, and your fingers had callouses. Your hair was still in a net, set in a shiny pompadour.

After a time I asked if I could play some guitar, seeing a beat-up steel string leaning against a wall. I was playing blues like the white guys did, and wanted to show off some speedy notes and phrases, and did a few riffs. You said, "Lemme show you something on that ax…" Muddy, you put it on your lap, and played a short blues phrase of four notes. Then played it again, slower, and louder, pulling the notes so they sounded painful. You said, with a warm smile, "That's blues, young man. Simple. Don't say too much. Blues is like life. Make each note feel."

That night I heard you play as if was the first time. You built up the pace to the moment when a note can twist you inside. The crowd went wild for you.

Muddy, Hoochie Coochie Man, you've been gone since 83, (hey, lived to 70). Paul died in 2021 from Covid, a very popular figure in the planet of blues that continues to this day. And there is this mural, high in the center of Chicago town, taller than a big oak tree. A giant in the skyline still bending that note on the guitar that taught me everything.

green rose cannabis dispensary

rose hidden in the ivy
shakespeare's noted weed
orchid of the beatnik jazz
thorns of divine paranoia
petals that the shaman smoked
whose extract fills the hookahs
with the mystical break

enlightenment offered
by a headless saint
dressed in blue satin
green rose of sativa

every day is earth day

our mother should praise our ingenuity
industry   technology   superiority
that we salute and adore her this day
lighting up a tower of waffled metals and glass
beyond dreams from the bibledoms of babylon
offering our obligatory hallmark card

we know our mother is wise beyond our years
she is not pleased and plans revenge
her patience wanes with every birth
as our population grows like weeds in a garden
each soul in need of computerized comforting
every day the future hardens

it is prophesied her plastic womb will erupt
to flood cities with oozy dunes from wild waves
bringing plagues from the corpses of rotten fish
as gasses from her bowels are spewed to an atmosphere
of oily sky burning in rays of grey sunlight
from sea to warming sea

alas when that passes we shall not be here
nor do we care   our generation   this civilization
the engine of commerce cannot be repaired
everything we earned would have to end
cell phones and satellites to be banned
and we return to till the land

truly she is to blame who begot us brats
the species that won her primal scheme
now we hunt for new planets to subdue
we children do what we must do
every day is earth day   dear mother
we will always love you

SW 14th Street murals

This Wall is Dope

you can't pull the trigger
if you don't have a gun

faces with traces
moustaches

have more fun
with AI
Artificial Indoctrination

aztec peyote poetry

alien
shapeshifters

Goofball
grim reaper

you get the idea...

wisp
we ♥ healthy vaginas
OUTFRONT
1316
IS
ANYONE'S GAME
THE WILDS

Ode to the Wonder of Womanhood
(We 🧡 Healthy Vaginas)

It is impossible to not concur,
for all of history, fig leaf or bare,
whether shaved or sculptured with hair,*
(*trigger warning for Evangelicals)
...inside or outside, no matter where,
as the old scroll says to our Tantric affairs:
a healthy one requires care.

Half of humanity surely understands,
more than we, who do not sit to pee,
but I can't pass this sign on Illinois
and not salute the women of Troy
who used the power of their sex
to stop a war for its delightful scents.

Wouldn't it be nice to see this ad
on the highways of Afghanistan?
Or Iran? Or Alabama-land?

Sanus amamus vaginas;
let it be in goldleaf above the portrait of Mary,
inscribed in odes to Danae.
As for the counterpart, lest we dismiss
the billboards boasting phallic precision—
sano amamus penis;
take steroids after circumcision.

PIER 31
31st Street Beachside Bar and Grill
"IF YOU CAN'T
GET TO MAUI,
YOU CAN ALWAYS
GET TO PIER 31"

A Nice Volcano to Visit

Dreams come true/In blue Hawaii
Songwriters: Leo Robin and Ralph Rainger

I

So many burnt alive on August 8, 2023,
Maui. The fire spread a mile minute
half a world away from Pier 31.

I was there thirty years ago in 1993,
to break up the New York winter;
I wanted to see with my own eyes,
this American fantasy called Hawaii:
tropical kingdoms of Polynesian myth,
skirt-wearing fishermen, forests of orchid.
Family time; let the kids smell the Pacific.

A very long flight. Too long. Maui.
Getting off the plane to the sound of Don Ho,
with a necklace of *aloha-flowers* placed
around my Hawaiian shirt by
a troupe of wonderful vibrating bellies;
I felt like an idiot....

Today Pier 31 is a most excellent beach,
with glass Lego block mountains in view,
a midsummer day by the Great Lake's
turquoise waves. Perfect for reading
on a folding chair, with drink in hand.
Who needs Maui?

But being the Windy City, it was windy,
and the umbrella refused to stay rooted,
dangerously jumping out from the soft sand
and almost spearing a passing jogger.
Then came the boom box with monotone whines
of rappers with that annoying wawa drawl,
as I read the news briefs on my cellphone

Ah, Maui!
It was a Gauguin paradise for centuries,
until Captain Cook introduced it to the court;
how fast all disappeared to sugar plantations
as all the native peoples on the earth
were baptized into slavery, (but not Christianity),
during the age of colonies to claim.
But now they are our fellow citizens,
with senators and golf courses,
stucco hotels, home of Pro Bowl,
Kona coffee and Maui Wowee marijuana—
buffet pu-pu platter and hula dance.
A Bollywood tale of gods at the luau;
maybe Las Vegas, but never Broadway.
Retire in the garden of the fiftieth state.
O those great big Hawaiian words
on the menus of the Tiki bars.

II

The firestorms raged like a bright tornado
across the digital screen in my palm.
Hundreds dead. A tempest of flames.
Haunting tales of last screams heard
by those burning alive.

III

There is no place safe on this planet now,
speculations of it all on the brink:
hot oceans, the dry cough of winds;
only the latest of heartbreaks to come.

I moved to a corner of the beach far
from the grill-smell of Pier 31
and read my journal from that time:

Haleakala Maui, Jan 10, 1993
A bike ride Jason and Evan will remember!
Started at dawn   dressed in layers
snow at the icy top   hot beaches below
a bicycle with no gears   downhill for an hour!
Softly down   breaking on smooth paths carved
on the side of an immense volcano
The foliage and rocks seemed to awake to the light
Different tropical zones   alien   green   thin air
soft winds of the Pacific
that whole ride was a state of mind
a meditation in cinemascope
a nice volcano to visit

That sign stares at me through the day
at the beach café at Pier 31.
I wonder if they will change it.
Maui is on fire, and heaven on earth,
sometimes, is where you happen to be.

UKRAINE

Women in Ukrainian Village

They come with a story to tell;
a journey through many continents,
sleeping on roads, hiding in trucks,
husbands and sons surviving or dead at the fronts,
with young children who are learning to smile.
Still half in nightmare; the sacrifices seem unreal.

They come with their wonderful accents
like they have lived here for decades,
blending in with the Chicago cold like professionals,
meeting at the local cafes for hot *compote*
with a slice of breakfast raison bread,
to talk about the traffic and kindergartens.

They take what work they can; once
executives are now helpers in a pastry shop—
they will walk dogs or mop the stairwells.
Some speak to the men on cellphones,
to hear the horrors and bravery,
fighting tears to the shudder of panic.

They come by the thousands but there are millions.
This they must live with, that they are here,
by fate alone, nothing that could be dreamed,
far from street killings and bombardments.
They are in the America that still offers hospitality,
unsure of the purpose that they survived
with days of highs and lows.

They sleep alone in queen size beds,
dreaming of their men.
They are here. Chicagoland.

PENNY
FOR YOUR
THOUGHTS?
- Murley.
WARNING

Vacant Lots and Condemned Dreams

Tell me wall, who begs for a penny,
asking me to stop the chatter of traffic
in my head, like Kant on his daily walks—
have you learned how to feel in the empty lot?
You want the stench of my thoughts?
They are with the weeds growing
from cracks in the pavement,
where no tree can root and offer shade—
where empty facades line the avenue
with a poverty of loneliness.

When I go out in this shithole city
the tents of the homeless hug in the underpass.
Buses arrive with refugees from the drug zones
beaten and battered with scars
and memories of hooded gangs;
car speakers play deafening drumbeats;
steam from the manholes in the gutter
sting the eyes with peppered tears;
the smokestacks drip urine from their spouts
and the whole empty lot stinks from it;
city of poverty, begging for handouts—
and you, wall, ask a *penny for my thoughts*?

Easy Come.
Easy go
13 FT 11 IN
NEXT 1 MIL

Easy come. Easy go.

Cliché, itself, is a cliché;
cliché is simply truth unbound;
cliché is never easy, never hard.
            Easy come. Easy go.

Way back when I had teeth and hair.
Now my jaw and head are bare.
Teeth and hair—overrated.
            Yessir. Easy come. Easy go.

What looms 13 ft 11 inches in a mile?
A goliath with a hatchet in his hand;
you better stay in your lane....
            Easy come....

Says here the universe is mostly dark matter:
dark energy sprinkled with gooey matter,
and something called matter-matter.
                Easy go....

Some guy set himself on fire.
Everybody took a selfie, complaining
you can't forget the stench—
            Easy bla-bla-bla

I could go on like this all day,
listen to operas by the weeping willow
touching my soul with teary falsetto.
            Easy peezy. Go schmo.

But you never get goosebumps
from the myth of Sisyphus,
now do you, Siri? Alexa?
            Easy, whatever.

Just Act on Your
Spicy Instinct!
NONGSHIM
SHIN

NONGSHIM
SHIN

acting on my instincts

my spicy instinct is my tongue on every nipple
my spicy instinct is to copulate like mountain peaks
the taste of salty saliva
scent of fig   arms and legs open like an albatross
chili peppers in the groin

my spicy instinct is chewing a warthog's still beating heart
after the kill   rip off its fur
put it in a fire pit with curry
and dance like a howling coyote

    but not
        a tiger by a midnight moon
            with a very weird expression
                like he's wacked out on opium
                    unable to get it up

my spicy instinct is not a bowl of noodles

Pure
Nostalgiahhhh
OLIPOP
ARKET

Fruit from the Nostalgia Tree

I was told not to bite or be filled with sadness—
refrain from sentimentality.
But nostalgia is born from a baobab tree
that has seen, has seen, has seen,
through its fruit with a thousand eyes.

It's well known you get addicted to it;
what does it matter to ease the pain?
I'm hopelessly hooked. I eat plentifully,
as it falls to the ground like crab apples,
best when overripe, that intoxicate to folly.

I hand pick my memories; my untamed youth
appears as tattoos, skin deep and fading
in this migration of sanctifying the now.
Lately I take a pill of tinctures from the pulp,
capsules packed with time release.

Ah, nostalgiahhhh!
The fruit alone has become acidic,
and the past can give you heartburn.

YOU.
COULD.
GO. ALL.
THE.
WAY.
BETRIVERS
SPORTSBOOK
EXCLUSIVE SPORTSBOOK PARTNER
OF THE CHICAGO BEARS

Syllabics of Gambling

You. Could. Go. All. The. Way.
Can't. Stop. And. Walk. A. Way.

Dreaming. Jackpots. Panic. Paybacks.
The rake. Is way. Above. Your pay.

Then again. Who's to say? If today. Is your day.
Count your coins. Contemplate. It's Lady Luck. To doomsday.

Losing streak blues. Ends at a wall. Behind the wall. Is just more wall.
Take opioids. Drink alcohol. Try slot machines. The lottery.

        Winner take all.
        You're tapped out.
        All the.
        Way.

42

-5° *at* 1:14

in minus five-degrees-grey the lake fades
on crooked lines of horizon
air is thick in waterfalls of ice
streets are ironstone
sidewalks are freezer zones

there are no shadows from streetlamps
lining avenues like witches' brooms
as the snow looks shot from splatter guns
and the

sky is semigloss sheetrock-white
above silhouettes of an old bottleshop
with facades of metal motherboards

i see my reflection in a storefront
bundlcd in layers of scarves
with two ridiculous hats and earmuffs
a ghost breathing like a chimney

winter in chicago is a bitch
even penguins avoid this fucking icebox
with its biting winds at highest pitch
this is my home now

About the Author:

Mark Fishbein (aka *Poet With Guitar*) was born in Brooklyn, NY. He got a BA in Literature from CCNY in 1970, and attended the Sorbonne in Paris for French Literature. Rejecting an academic life, he found a career in the flourishing screen printing and t-shirt dyeing industry, raising a family in NYC, always "with a book of poems in his pocket." In 2018, Mark left the industry and immediately re-engaged with poetry.

Mark has five books and has published in a variety of journals from the *Hill Rag* to the *American Atheist Magazine*. His most recent work, "Reflections in the Time of Trumpius Maximus," is a collection of 50 political poems written 2016-2021 (Atmosphere Press, 2021). He also has translated a collection by the French poet Paul Eluard, among others.

Online, Mark is host to weekly writers workshops, and a unique Zoom event, Planet Poetry 28, a monthly virtual magazine introducing poets from around the world who perform their poetry while showing the work on Share Screen.

Mark is on the ExeCom of PGN-Poetry Global Network. He is Chancellor of "The Poetry Academy," which offers workshops and study events focusing of subjects of interest to the modern Zoom generation of poets.

Mark is currently enrolled in Columbia College, Chicago, for an MFA in Poetry, to make teaching the final engagement of his life.

After decades of self-taught playing, Mark took up classical guitar in 2000 and currently plays professionally at art openings, poetry readings, weddings etc. He often combines his poetry reading with his eclectic music style.

He now lives in Chicago with his wife Elaine, whom he met in a protest rally against the war in Vietnam. They have two sons and three grandchildren.

Mark@poetwithguitar.com, or www.poetwithguitar.com

9 798869 325617